Maurizio Eliseo

Six Stars on the Ocean
SEVEN SEAS NAVIGATOR
A dream cruise ship for the 21st Century

Carmania Press
London, 2001

Contents

Foreword

Dear Fellow Navigator,

You are holding in your hand a work of art within a work of art. The *Seven Seas Navigator* stands apart from other ships as the furthest advancement of the shipbuilder's art. It reasons, then that this book, which seeks to capture its beauty, must therefore also qualify.

At the *Navigator*'s launch, I had the honor to be named Godmother of the ship. A more beautiful and wonderful godchild could not be wished for. Enjoy your time aboard her, and sail home with memories of incomparable amenities and service by a professional cruise staff which seeks only to please. This is the goal of every Seven Seas cruise experience.

During the launch, I bequeathed a verse to my godchild, and I'd like to share it with you now;

Through starlit nights and dappled days,
Pray we o' Navigator
Safe lead our way
Sail our souls to distant shores
That touch and change us, evermore.

Welcome aboard!

Marilyn Carlson Nelson
Chairman & CEO
Carlson Companies

The Builders

Founded in 1928 by the ship repairer Temistocle Mariotti in the Italian port of Genoa, the builders of the *Seven Seas Navigator* have more than 70 years of experience of the shipbuilding and marine outfitting fields. In particular, they have shown great skill and ingenuity in the rebuilding and refitting of passenger ships.

Mariotti came to prominence in this field in the early 'sixties with two important conversions. In 1961-62 the French ship *Lavoisier* was completely revamped and refitted, both in her exterior appearance and in her interior décor, to become the cruise ship *Riviera Prima,* a pioneer of the modern full-time cruise market. The following year Mariotti undertook the conversion of the British *Empress of Britain* into the Greek flagship *Queen Anna Maria*.

T. Mariotti has grown over the years, diversifying its activities, and can now boast a full range of technical services to the marine industry, from the planning stages to the actual construction. The present shipyard, built ex-novo in 1994 in a new area of the port of Genoa, covers repairs, outfitting, building and conversion of vessels of all types, as well as maintenace and installation of machinery, engines and mechanical equipment. It has won worldwide renown and its name is linked to some of the most luxurious and succesful cruise ships now sailing.

From research to design, and from the management to the production workforce, the value of the "human resource" is one of the basic factors behind the company's success.

More than seventy years of experience in one of the busiest ports in the world, a nerve centre of Mediterranean shipping, has been inherited by the younger members of the design and building team.

This, together with continuous training and updating, allows the Mariotti shipyard to blend the modern drive of a large worldwide-oriented company with the unique qualities of craftsmen proud of their tradition and origins. In more recent years Mariotti has dramatically invested in new premises and offers a modern shipyard of 20,000 square metres of which 6,000 are covered and occupied by offices, workshops and stores. Specialist divisions for pipe-work, mechanics and carpentry are available within the shipyard and this, in association with high technology facilities and skilled manpower, means cost-cutting and time-saving with an improved production quality. Furthermore, the Mariotti shipyard is close to the dry-docks of the port, able to take vessels up to 100,000 dwt.

The brand new *Seven Seas Navigator* has been the latest proof of the great success achieved by Mariotti in its long life and the superb standard of her interiors together with the overall quality of the building are a real tribute to the craftmanship, the dedication and love which always characterise the vessels built by this shipyard. But perhaps the best tribute remains the fact that a larger version of the *Seven Seas Navigator*, to be called the *Seven Seas Voyager*, has been ordered from Mariotti in the Fall of 2000.

Above: the new premises of T. Mariotti, opened in 1994 and, *right*, the old headquarters, recently demolished during the radical modernisation and reconstruction of the port of Genoa.

Below: the *Riviera Prima*, first cruise ship converted by T. Mariotti in 1962 and the *Queen Anna Maria*, the Greek flagship which was a 1963 conversion of the former *Empress of Britain*.

Through close alliances with other firms in the field but with Mariotti acting as overall directors of operations, a high degree of service integration is achieved. In this way, a large project such as the building of the *Seven Seas Navigator* can be successfully completed and economies of scale can be achieved.

The Owners

On 13th August 1998 Radisson Seven Seas Cruises officially announced the expansion of its fleet of luxury cruise ships with a spacious and elegantly designed vessel, the *Seven Seas Navigator*.

This all-suite, luxurious new flagship of 30,000 gross tons accommodates only 490 guests, with an exceptional passenger/crew ratio of 1.5, and "reflects precisely what guests have told Radisson Seven Seas Cruises they want", according to her Godmother, Mrs Marilyn Carlson Nelson.

The *Seven Seas Navigator* is actually jointly owned by the Monaco-based V.Ships, one of the largest shipping management companies in the world, founded in 1928 and with a half-century of experience in the passenger ship sector, and Radisson Seven Seas, already acknowledged as one of the few top-market cruise companies, and covering hundreds of exclusive itineraries and destinations all over the world.

Radisson Seven Seas Cruises is one of the youngest of the cruise operators but it has a wealth of experience behind it. Already it is among the largest luxury lines in the world and has established a fine reputation for its exclusive cruises. Headquartered in Fort Lauderdale, Florida, it is part of Carlson Hospitality Worldwide, a major group with 1,200 hotels, resorts, restaurants and cruise ships. The Carlson Group includes Radisson Hotels Worldwide, Regent International Hotels, Country Inns & Suites By Carlson, Carlson Restaurants Worldwide (including TGI Friday's and eight other restaurant brands), plus Provisions, a global procurement company. In 1998 total revenues of Carlson brands amounted to $22 billion.

With a total capacity of over 1,500 berths, Radisson Seven Seas Cruises operates and markets, apart from the *Seven Seas Navigator*, the Six-Star, 350-guest *Radisson Diamond*; the 180-guest *Song of Flower*, and the 320-guest *Paul Gauguin,* all ships which carry relatively small numbers of passengers in great comfort. The company also markets the Five-Star *Hanseatic*, the most luxurious adventure cruise ship in the world.

Furthermore, as part of its continuous expansion programme, Radisson Seven Seas Cruises ordered, in December 1998, a brand-new ultra-luxury vessel of 50,000 gross registered tons. A product of the French yard Chantiers de l'Atlantique and to be named *Seven Seas Mariner,* she is due to be delivered in February 2001. And another similar vessel, the *Seven Seas Voyager*, has been ordered from Mariotti.

Already, with its present fleet, Radisson Seven Seas Cruises can boast a long list of awards and honours. In 1995 Condé Nast Traveler's "Readers Choice Awards" named the company "World's Best Cruise Line" and in 1998 the "Best Value In Luxury Cruising" award was given to them by "Cruise Critic U.S.A.".

Individual RSSC ships have won honours from such authoritative sources as Fielding's Guide to Worldwide Cruises and Stern's Travel Guides, getting the Six Star Rating and the Six Black Ribbon Rating, the most exclusive honour a cruise ship can achieve.

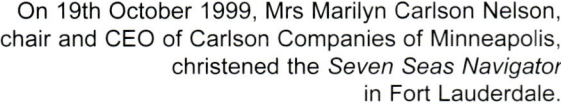

On 19th October 1999, Mrs Marilyn Carlson Nelson, chair and CEO of Carlson Companies of Minneapolis, christened the *Seven Seas Navigator* in Fort Lauderdale.

To name the ship, the godmother used a "magic wand" presented to her for the occasion. One of the twenty most powerful women in American business, Mrs Nelson is known by the International Press as "America's First Lady of Travel".

On the left, the group of authorities attending the ceremony and Mr Mark Conroy, President and CEO of RSSC, during his speech on board.

Two ceremonies for a future of great success

Only a few months after the christening of
the *Seven Seas Navigator*, another ceremony took place
which underlined the great public success
of the vessel and her owners.
On 3rd April 2000 the first block of
the *Seven Seas Mariner*, a similar but larger
version of the *Seven Seas Navigator* was
laid in the building dock of
Chantiers de L'Atlantique in St. Nazaire, France.
A 100 French Francs silver coin was put inside the double
bottom of the newbuilding to celebrate the event and as a
good omen for the future flagship
of Radisson Seven Seas Cruises.

A new fleet-mate for the *Seven Seas Navigator*: on 9th September 2000 the *Seven Seas Mariner* was launched and towed to the fitting-out berth.

The Radisson Seven Seas Fleet

SSC RADISSON DIAMOND

The 20,200 gross tons *Radisson Diamond*, completed in 1992, combines small-ship intimacy with large-ship amenities. Her instantly recognisible profile springs from her twin-hull design, which cuts down on pitching and rolling movements. Of her 177 spacious staterooms, all overlooking the sea, 123 feature private balconies. From December through April she operates a distinctive Trans Panama Canal programme featuring Costa Rica and the Caribbean, while her Summers are devoted to Mediterranean and Baltic cruises.

M/S SONG OF FLOWER

The 8,300 gross tons *Song of Flower*, renowned for her yachtlike ambience, Scandinavian refinement and destination-intensive explorations of exotic ports, sails seasonally to India, the Red Sea, Arabia and the Far East, including China, Burma, Vietnam and Indonesia, with summers spent exploring classic Mediterranean, Scandinanvian, Baltic and Northern European destinations. She has a capacity of 180 guests in 100 staterooms, all with outside views and 10 with private verandas. Her European crew numbers 144.

M/S PAUL GAUGUIN

The 19,200 gross tons *Paul Gauguin* was built in France and delivered in December, 1997. She started on her maiden cruise on 31st January 1998 and is the most de luxe cruise ship ever to be based year-round in Polynesia. Providing six star accommodation for just 320 guests, her 160 staterooms and suites are all outside and half of them have private balconies. In particular, there are seven suites, varying from 300 to 457 square feet. Among the exclusive facilitie provided is a state-of-the-art retractable watersports marina.

M/S HANSEATIC

The 9,000 gross tons *Hanseatic* is owned by the German Hapag Lloyd but chartered for Antartica cruises by Radisson Seven Seas Cruises. The Five-Star vessel offers a unique way to discover rarely-visited parts of the world. A real "Adventure Cruise Ship", the *Hanseatic* was rated one of the ten "Best Bets" for nature lovers by Fielding's Guide to Worldwide Cruising. She has a capacity of 184 guests in 90 large staterooms and a crew of 125 members.

The design

A ship is like a city. One of the most complex scientific design achievements of man. To understand this statement it should be realised that when a vessel sails in the open sea with her precious cargo of human beings, she needs to be self-sufficient in every way. She must produce energy to move, to communicate, to provide water, food and every comfort for the people who live inside her shell and all in the safest way.

A ship like the *Seven Seas Navigator* is more than a high technology project; she is a floating village where 1000 people can live, relax, enjoy the voyage and work. The designers must first of all transform the preliminary idea of a client, in this case the shipowner, into a series of technical documents, drawings and specifications which allow the construction of such an object.

The more complex the design, the greater the number of technical documents to be prepared, compared and studied before arriving at the final decisions. Almost 13,000 drawings, enough to cover a dozen football fields, were made during the design stage of the *Seven Seas Navigator*.

The net of people who prepared, checked and approved the designs for the *Seven Seas Navigator* were the members of the V.Ships Leisure Newbuilding Department, to whom the Owners entrusted the co-ordination of the whole project, from the early stage of planning to the vessel's delivery.

The origins of the concept design of the vessel were the preliminary specification and General Arrangement Plans agreed between Radisson Seven Seas Cruises and V.Ships. The aim was to produce a vessel of the highest standard on the market, a "Six Star Ship", capable of providing hospitality to 490

The body plan of the ship here illustrated is one of the building drawings of the hull of the *Seven Seas Navigator*. It was originally traced by hand, being still nowadays one of the few drawings that cannot be computer-generated. The hull of a ship is like a work of art, designed to cope with the sea and an object of deep study to give speed, steadiness and stability in any condition of weather. Starting from the body plan, a scale model of the vessel is built to undergo a series of tests in a tank where the model is towed, simulating the real situation at sea. The model is built in wood and is sanded down to the smallest detail. With applications of wax it is later possible to correct the shape where necessary in order to obtain a perfect balance of forms and the minimum resistance during navigation.

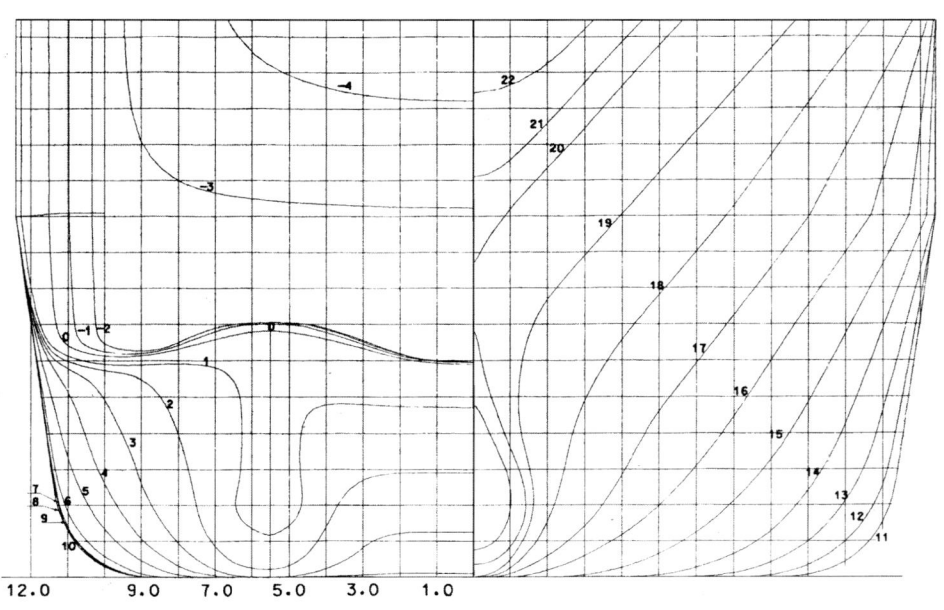

passengers and 400 crew members. These figures indicated a very high ratio of crew to passengers in line with the company's policy of offering its guests the most attentive service.

The world-renowned firm of Yran and Storbraaten, architects from Oslo, were entrusted with the design of the tasteful interiors and décor. They created an intimate atmosphere with different shades of pastel colours on the ceilings and in the carpets, precious veined marbles and stones, different types of wood on the walls, enriched by specially-designed lamps and fabrics. The vessel was designed to give the maximum natural light possible, entering through large windows and deck-to-deck glass walls. No ordinary ship, the *Seven Seas Navigator* occupies the uppermost niche in cruising, the entire navigable world being at her command.

Stepping on board the vessel one is immediately struck by the sheer elegance of her interiors and surprised by her range of rooms, both public spaces and private suites.

The vessel actually has no "cabins" but only generously large suites, ranging from more than 300 square feet to over 1,170, each with rich damasks and sumptuous silks in the shades of sand and terra-cotta. The soft fabrics are set off by warmly finished woods and all suites are exterior with sweeping ocean views.

With a passenger space ratio of 61.2 the *Seven Seas Navigator* is one of the most spacious ships sailing the seas. In designing the interior space of the vessel the architects were inspired by Einstein's motto "space is curve". In fact, from the beginning an expansive view greets the guests who enter the soaring Atrium. Curvilinear walls of glass and stairways cantilevering into a vast column of vertical space give the sensation of being liberated from the constraints of earth. Spiraling walkways criss-cross the Atrium like stairways to

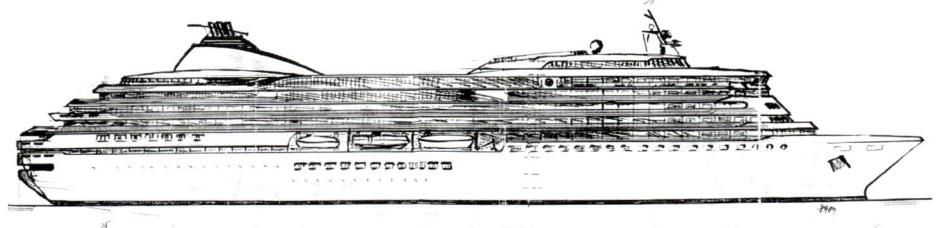

One of the preliminary sketches by the architects showing the intended profile of the *Seven Seas Navigator* during an early stage of design and, below, the definitive one.

the stars, while glass-walled elevators rise through deck upon deck of airy lounges to the Solarium and the Lido Area. On this ship the guests are reminded of the opulence of the great Ocean Liners of the 'twenties and of the 'thirties with the feeling present in every corner of the "International Streamline Style"; sweeping railings of wood and chromed steel and bevelled glass panels are softened by yards of silken draperies. Sculptured friezes and original murals grace curving walls punctuated by carved niches displaying intriguing works of art.

On the *Seven Seas Navigator* every modern comfort is to be found; inspired by the grandeur of floating palaces of the past, she is however a vessel of the 21st Century. No more endless corridors of cabin doors, noisy and crowded reception area and bothersome announcements to interrupt the feeling of relaxation on board; she is a remarkably personal ship: all is calm and quiet, as in a small de-luxe hotel where all guests are considered friends and not names or numbers. The surroundings of the public area are as intimate as a private club.

The passenger accommodation is situated on ten of the fourteen decks of the vessel. To enable passengers to embark easily at any of the ports at which the vessel might call, three different decks are fitted with shell doors and their own vestibule. In addition, on deck 4, there is the tender embarkation area to bring the passenger ashore while the ship is anchored in a roadstead; the *Seven Seas Navigator* has two 150-passenger tenders in addition to four lifeboats.

The public rooms are on decks 6, 7 and 12, exception made for the Compass Rose restaurant, placed on deck 5, and for the Panorama Lounge high up on deck 11, while the suites occupy the whole of decks 8 and 9 and the forward portion of the upper ones. On board, the passenger flow develops around the central hall, which spans from deck 4 to deck 12 and is served by three panoramic lifts. Additionally, there is a stern staircase with another two lifts. Deck 6 contains the main reception, the card room, the conference room, the cigar lounge "Connoisseur Club", the Navigator Club bar and the library and reading room, while on the upper deck are located the casino and the shopping gallery. From the aft part of the latter deck, passengers gain access to the two-level "Seven Seas" show lounge. A part of the lower level of the show lounge acts also as night club and disco with its own bar for late bird passengers. The stern portion of deck 11 is occupied by the "Galileo's" Panorama Lounge, a quiet place with soothing soft music, deck to deck glass walls facing the sea and where early risers can grab a cup of coffee and a croissant.

Another point of attraction for passengers is deck 12, completely devoted to the health center, fitted with gymnasium, massage rooms, thalasso theraphy, turkish bath and sauna. At the forward end the fitness center opens into the "Vista" Observation Lounge, a relaxing place with a panoramic view similar to that of the bridge, located one deck below. The Vista Lounge is actually fitted with some wheel-house instrument repeaters, such as GPS, map, speed and route indicator and other screens giving meteorological and navigating information, so that interested passengers may follow the ship's progress.

The *Seven Seas Navigator* is one of the very first cruise ships to be designed with the so-called "full green concept"; thanks to her "state-of-the-art" sewage and garbage treatment system, she complies with the most restrictive rules for pollution prevention and can sail anywhere in the world, including special protected areas. She is a very versatile vessel: not conceived for repetitive cruises but to navigate the seven seas, the new cruise ship carries enough provisions to last six weeks and has a range of 7,500 miles at cruising speed.

The *Seven Seas Navigator* is fitted with
two controllable-pitch propellers manufactured by
the famous firm of KaMeWa.
Several models were tested in the cavitation tank
at Hamburg in order to determine the best shape
and design so as to give the maximum speed and
performace possible, while reducing noise and
vibration to a minimum.

The funnel shape of a vessel is always the subject of careful design and testing.
Apart from contributing to the distinctive appearance of the ship, it is very important that the exhaust gases from the engine room and auxiliary plants do not fall on the open decks. These studies are performed in a wind tunnel, where also the so-called comfort test is performed. The latter allows the optimization of the upperworks shape and the fitting of windscreens in order to prevent strong flows of air on the open decks and the lido area.

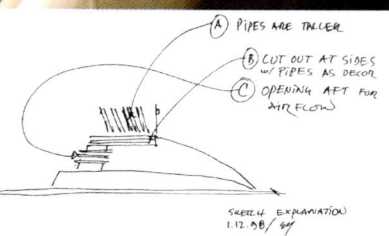

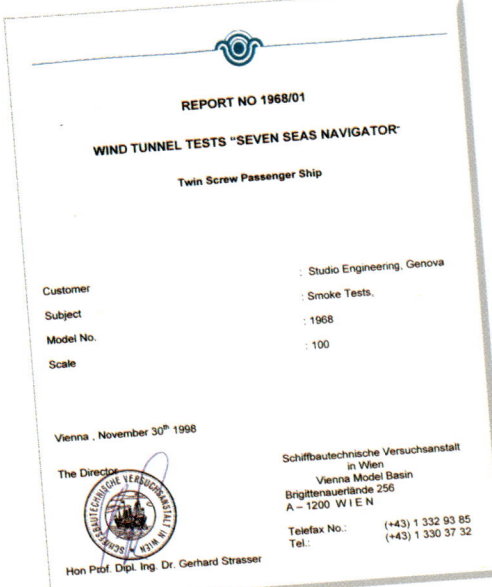

REPORT NO 1968/01

WIND TUNNEL TESTS "SEVEN SEAS NAVIGATOR"

Twin Screw Passenger Ship

Customer	: Studio Engineering, Genova
Subject	: Smoke Tests.
Model No.	: 1968
Scale	: 100

Vienna , November 30th 1998

The Director

Schiffbautechnische Versuchsanstalt
in Wien
Vienna Model Basin
Brigittenauerlände 256
A – 1200 W I E N

Telefax No.: (+43) 1 332 93 85
Tel.: (+43) 1 330 37 32

Hon Prof. Dipl. Ing. Dr. Gerhard Strasser

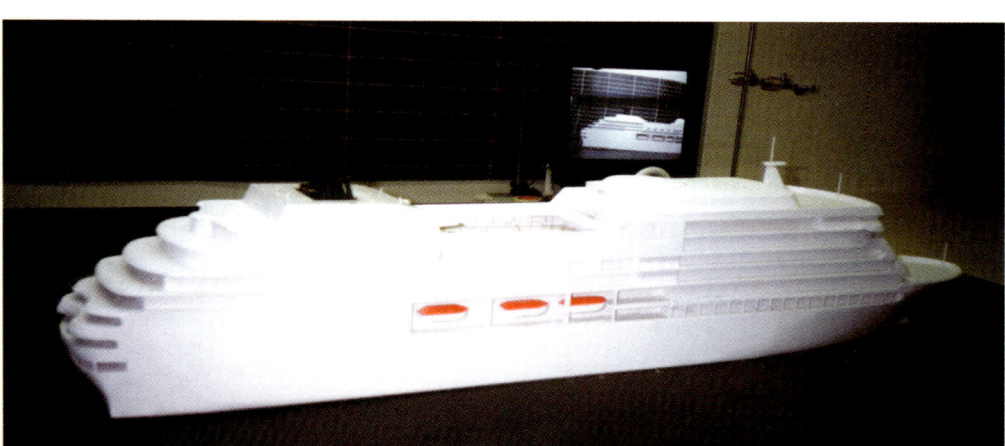

Wind test & funnel design

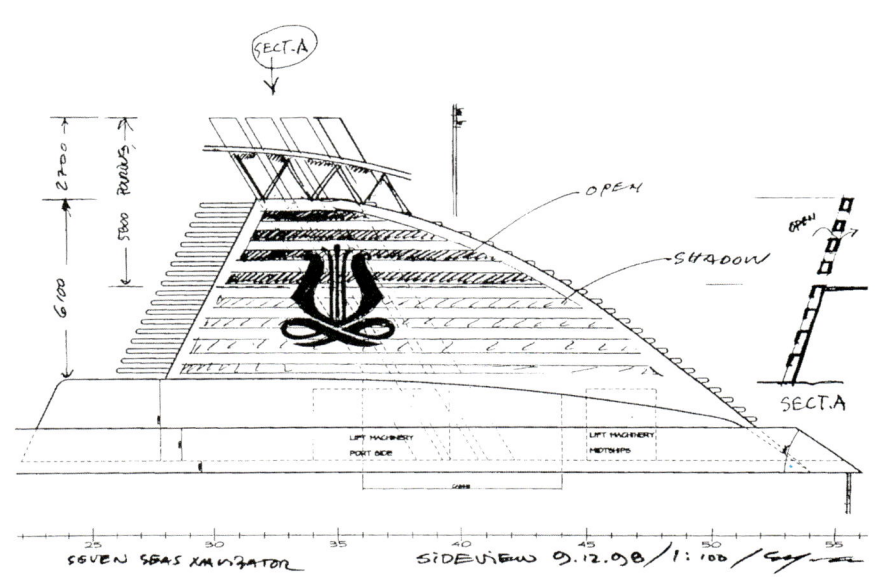

SEVEN SEAS NAVIGATOR   SIDEVIEW 9.12.98/1:100

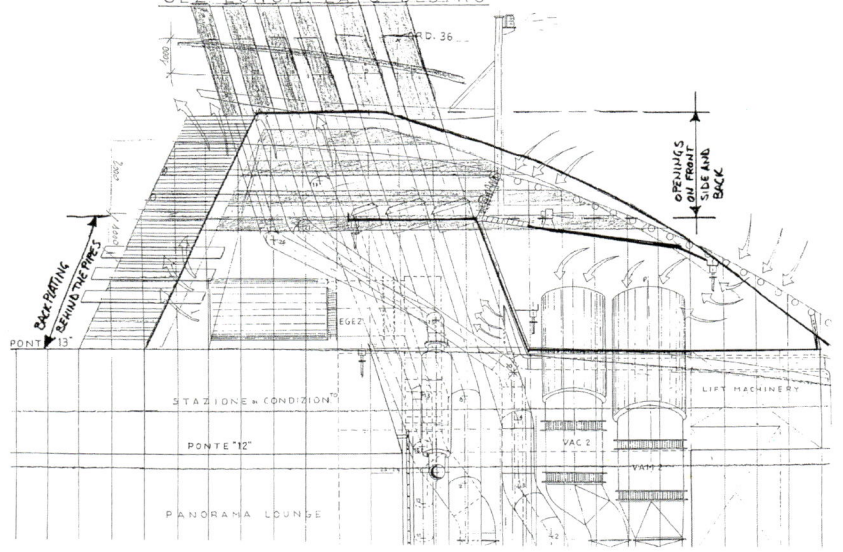

SEZ LONGIT LATO DESTRO

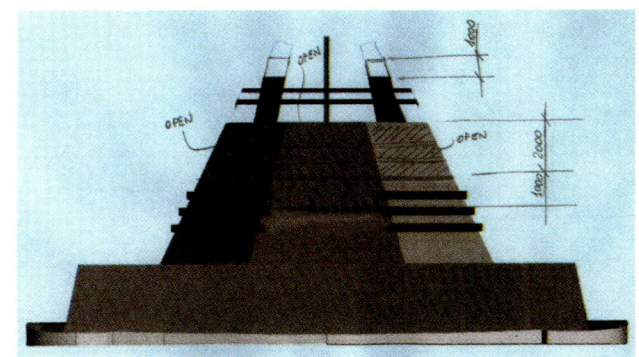

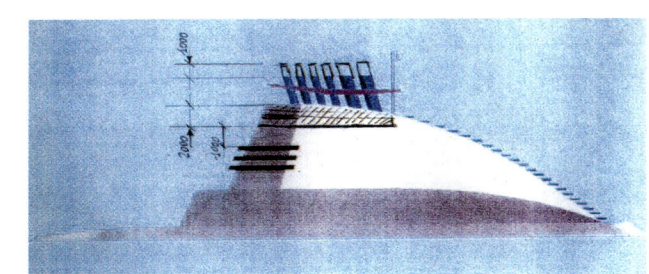

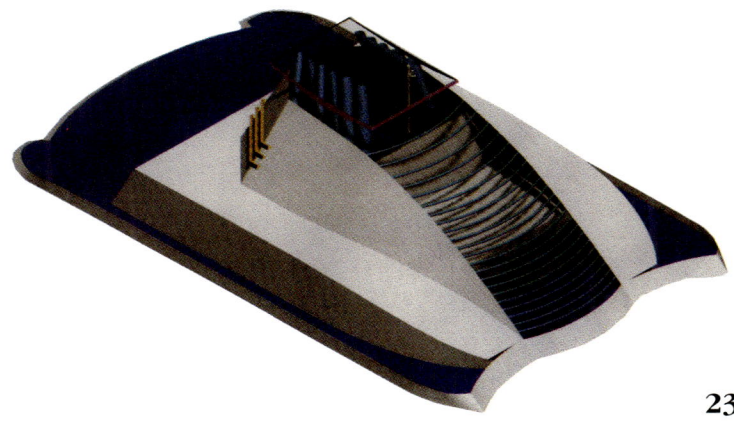

Building a Seven Seas Navigator

As in all modern cruise ships, the steel hull of the *Seven Seas Navigator* is integrated with the superstructure, which is built of aluminium alloy. The bow has an underwater bulbous form and is designed to sail safely also through icy seas, thanks to the special strength given to the hull structure.

The stern is of cruiser type with tiers of graceful balconies enabling the passengers to enjoy the seascape, particularly from the upper Portofino Grill Restaurant.

The overall length of the vessel is 170.60 m (559.7 ft) while the length between perpendiculars is 150.00 m (492.1 ft); her moulded breadth is 24.80 m (81.4 ft) and the normal draft 6.9 metres (23 ft).

The very latest technology has been used in building the superstructure and has resulted in a considerable saving of weight. The traditional beams and other stiffeners have been integrated into the extruded aluminium panels which form the deck plating. These have enabled the designers to raise the ceilings of the rooms and create a more spacious feeling.

Under the supervision of RINA (Registro Italiano Navale), the hull and every other aspect of the *Seven Seas Navigator* have been designed and built to conform with the very strict new safety regulations, known as SOLAS 2000. In addition, Radisson Seven Seas Cruises has been particularly anxious that their new ship should comply fully with the various regulations which protect the environment.

The *Seven Seas Navigator* can thus be said to be a thoroughly "green ship" and can take her passengers to the most breathtaking areas forbidden to the majority of cruise ships.

She is also a vessel with a very long range; she has sufficient capacity for fuel, water and provisions to enable her to sail for 7,500 miles and at least six weeks without needing to be re-stocked. She is thus ideal for long cruises and world-wide itineraries.

While the hull of the vessel lies at the fitting out quay, new parts of the superstructure and top houses are welded together and assembled before being lifted by the giant crane and put in position on board.

An echoing cathedral of steel waiting to be filled.
This is the first impression obtained by the
observer who walks through the decks of the ship
before her outfitting begins.
Vast and ample metal floors and walls wait
for the finished decorative panels to be fitted.
The holes in the beams are also clearly
visible; apart from lightening the ship's weight
these holes will be used for the passage
of electrical cables, pipes and air ducts hidden
behind the counter-ceiling, which will thus
be invisible to the passengers.

The empty structure of the bridge during an early stage of construction and, below, the finished wheel-house; the state-of-the-art technology bridge is the nerve centre of the vessel, like a brain from which all the commands concerning the navigation and the running of the ship start.

Some phases of the outfitting of the Navigator Show Lounge and, below, the metal structure of the balconies before the outfitting begins.

The propulsion plant

The propelling machinery of the *Seven Seas Navigator* is based on a Diesel propulsion system. Each of the two shafts is driven by a couple of Wärtsilä 8L/38 internal combustion engines. The shaft horse power of the vessel is 14,600 HP, giving a service speed of 19.5 knots. Through a gear unit each shaft also drives a 2,500 kW electrical generator, supplying the energy for the on-board services together with another three Wärtsilä-Vasa/Leroy-Somer 6R32 diesel-generators of 2,000 kW each.
At full speed the ship reaches 21 knots.
To facilitate the manoeuvrability of the ship, apart from the variable-pitch propellers and the couple of twin rudders, the *Seven Seas Navigator* is fitted with two bow thrusters of 500 kW each.

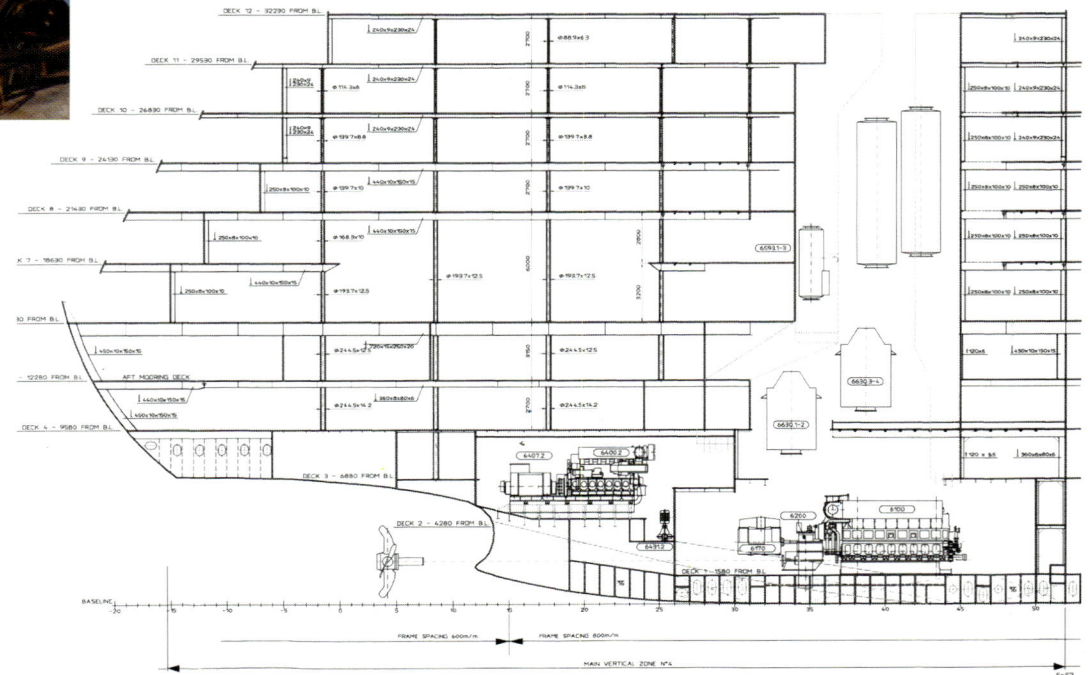

On 12th May 1998, the hull of the *Seven Seas Navigator* entered drydock in Genoa for the fitting of the stern and of the seats to house the main diesel engines and the diesel-generators.

Power plant and main auxiliaries

Main Engines: 4 Wärtsilä 8L38
5280 kW each - 600 rpm

Service speed: 19.5 knots

Auxiliary engines: 3 Wärtsilä R32LND
2,120 kW each - 720 rpm

Shaft alternators: 2 Leroy Somer LSA 56 A
2,500 kW each - 1800 rpm

Propellers: 2 KaMeWa CPS 130/4
Ø 4,600 mm - 120 rpm

Bow Thruster: 2 Proletarsky - 500 kW each

Fin Stabilisers:
2 Fincantieri SRO-3-110

Garbage handling system: Isir/Pyrall

Biological Sewage treatment plant:
Isir "Bioepuro" B250

Sewage collecting units:
Isir/Jets Vacuum 120MB

Automation: ABB

Integrated Navigation System:
NACOS 719
STN Atlas Elektronik Multiplot 9106

Air Conditioniong Plant:
Atisa centralized HVAC enthalpy
recovery system with cabin
individual control and re-heating system

Engine Control Room

The engine room,
heart of the ship

The upper decks, such as deck 9 shown in the picture above, are built in light aluminium alloy, to reduce weight. This space will house the Navigator Suites, with large deck-to-deck windows and verandas overlooking the sea. The stairs, for safety reasons, are built in steel like the vertical trunk in which they are fitted.
As in modern land buildings, fire doors separate the stair trunks from the rest of the decks, in order to protect the area from smoke in case of fire,
thus permitting an easy and quick evacuation.
In case of danger each fire door, kept open through a magnet stopper, can be closed by a local release-switch or from the bridge.

The elegantly dressed passenger who now descends the stairs into the Compass Rose Restaurant or who gazes at the towering atrium from one of its balconies, would find it difficult to recognise the same rooms in these pictures, showing the massive steelwork which lies behind the handsome décor.

The central atrium is served by three panoramic lifts;
it is based on a network of curvilinear walls, stairs and platforms which cross all passenger decks up to the Solarium's windows, from where
natural light enters to flood the space.

The sun produces a striking pattern of light and shade as the abstract design of the architects becomes a shapely reality in the hands of the experienced shipyard workers.

Seven hundred kilometres of cables are tidily laid on board the *Seven Seas Navigator*, many of them hidden in the ceilings.

A capillar net through which the 8,000 kW of electricity produced on board is distributed to every corner of the ship, as well as the signals for telephones, television, music, smoke-detectors, remote controlled devices, etc.

A huge job which can be successfully realised through careful design and subsequent execution of the co-ordination drawings.

The distinctive funnel casing, already prefabricated ashore together with its housing, is lifted into its final position.

The *Seven Seas Navigator* is equipped with 5 lifts
for passengers, and 2 for the crew and for goods.
They are of special type, robust and reliable,
in order to withstand the continuous stress of the
ship's structure and the sudden movements
which can occur with rough seas.
In the photograph, the panoramic lifts are
undergoing a series of tests by
specialised technicians
from the manufacturers.

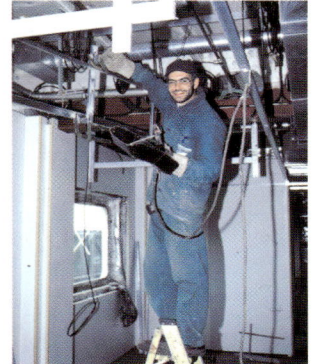

When all the cabling, piping and air-ducts have been fitted and tested, the decorative ceiling panels are put in position. Like any other element on board a vessel, these panels must comply with many requirements; they must be fire-, noise- and vibration- proof but also be easily removable to gain access to the plants and controls they hide.
The fitting of the specially designed carpet, tested and approved by the classification society, indicates that the outfitting of the ship is close to its end.

The final touches.
Inside the ship, workmen finish off
one of the shops and make final
adjustments to ceiling panels, while,
outside,
the deck carpet is laid.

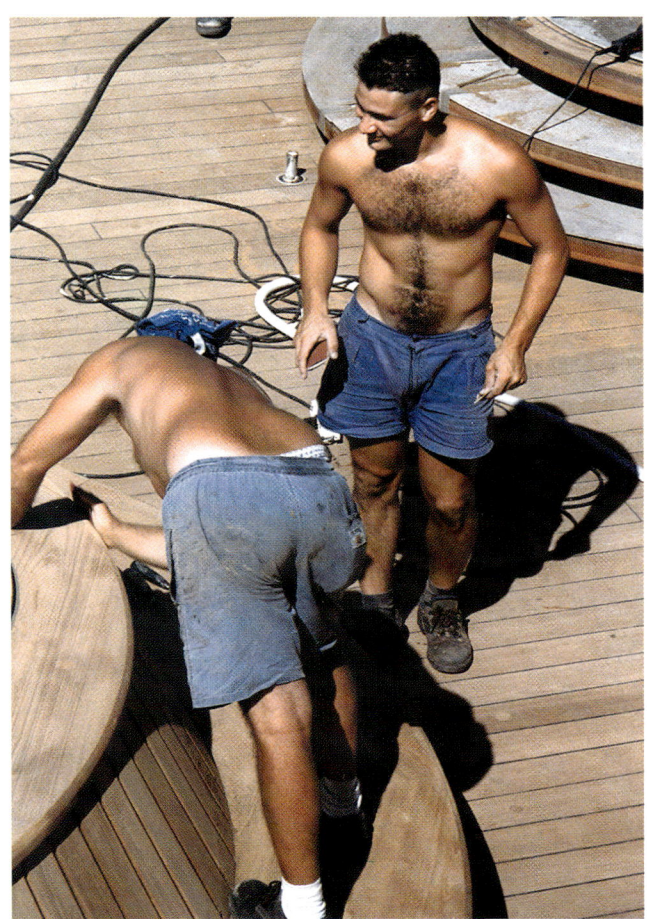

During the very last phases of
outfitting, the deck coverings
are being finished.
All outside passenger decks,
including the balconies of the suites,
are clad with 2-inch thick teak.
Meanwhile, the mooring decks are
painted blue.

As the ship is made ready for service,
several tons of plastic coverings,
cardboard and other protective
materials are removed
and carefully disposed of.

The last of the scaffolding is taken down.

Thanks to modern technology, a simple joystick on the bridge answers to the touch of a finger; via a powerful computer, it manoeuvres the giant ship, acting on the rudders, on the pitch of the propellers and on the bow-thrusters.

In August 1999 the *Seven Seas Navigator* was drydocked for a final check of these devices and of the fin stabilisers; she was also given a final coat of protective paint before being floated out again.

The floating out

49

A close-up view of the portside lifeboat and tenders suspended over the promenade; and (previous page) another fine shot of the Seven Seas Navigator during her last pre-delivery dry-dock.

In their nests lifted by cranes,
the painters give the final touches by hand, while the
raised letters of the name get their
royal blue colour.

Sea Trials

"Remove gangway, let go ropes!"
With these orders from the bridge,
the last connections between the ship
and the wharf are removed.
For the first time
the vessel is totally free
and enters her element.

On 23rd July 1999, a beautiful Summer morning, the *Seven Seas Navigator*,
carefully asssisted by tugs, leaves the
shipyard and is towed out of the ancient port of Genoa, dominated by the famous "Lanterna", the medieval light-tower, symbol of the city; for the first time she enters the crystal blue sea of the Gulf of Genoa, where she will run her successful sea trials.

During and after the sea trials a small
army of people is at work
to prepare the vessel
for her first guests.
The last finishes are given, while
thousands of signs are put in
position and the crew cleans and
polishes every corner,
co-ordinated by the ship's officers and
the owner's superintendents.

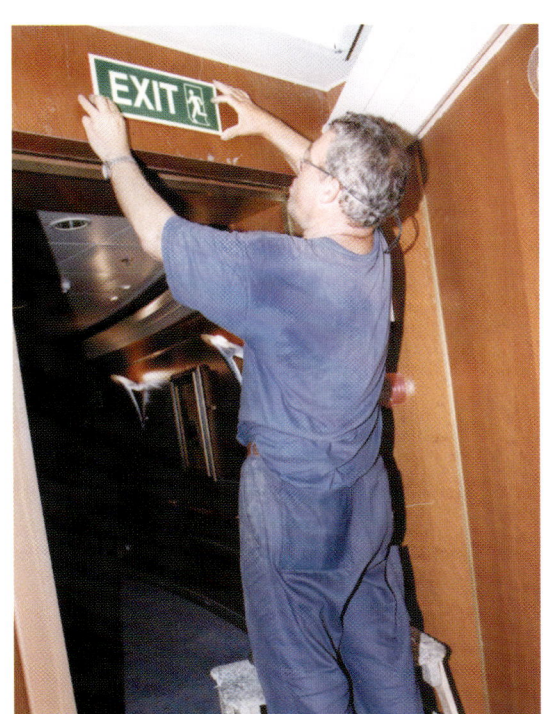

On 28th August 1999,
the delivery ceremony
in Genoa marked the start
of a series of introductory
ceremonies which ended
in Fort Lauderdale, Florida,
on the following
19th October, with
the official christening by the
Seven Seas Navigator's
godmother,
Mrs Marilyn Carlson Nelson
who smashed the traditional
bottle of champagne
on the ship's side.

Delivery and maiden voyage

Time to go! All lit up, the *Seven Seas Navigator* is ready to start her undocking manoeuvre and her midnight sailing to Nice, along the beautiful Riviera, where her first guests wait to welcome her.

Magic pictures capture the atmosphere as
the *Seven Seas Navigator*,
lit overall, leaves the port of Genoa on her
maiden cruise, saluted by
the magnificent show of the city at night and
under a sky of twinkling stars
and a beautiful red half-moon;
it is 1st September 1999.

Nice, on the famous French Riviera, was the first call of the vessel during her maiden cruise; in the evening the first sumptuous gala dinner was held for the authorities and the press.

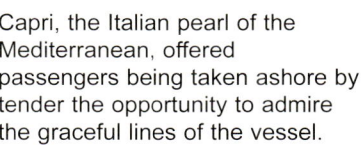

Capri, the Italian pearl of the Mediterranean, offered passengers being taken ashore by tender the opportunity to admire the graceful lines of the vessel.

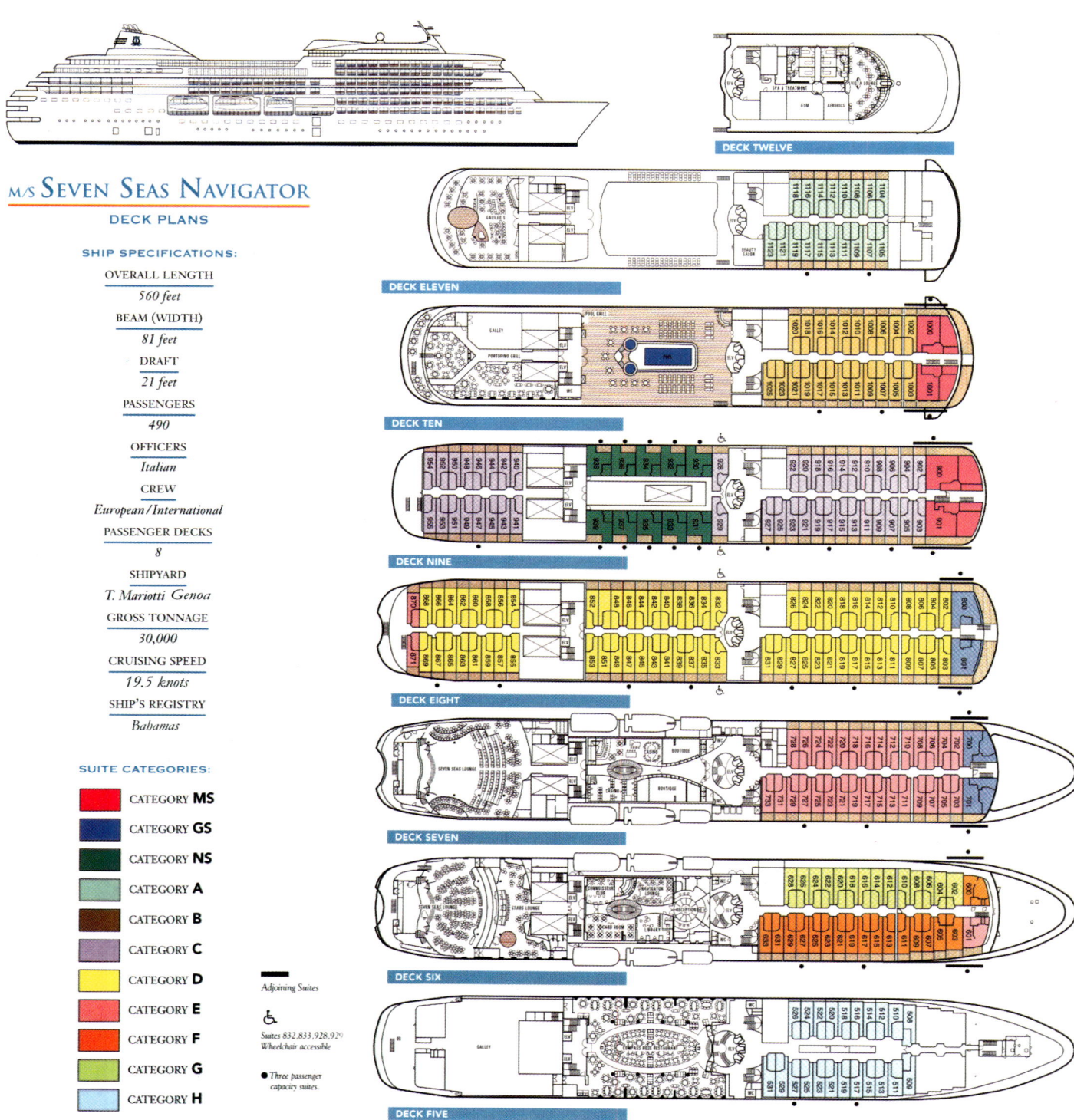

M/S SEVEN SEAS NAVIGATOR

DECK PLANS

SHIP SPECIFICATIONS:

OVERALL LENGTH
560 feet

BEAM (WIDTH)
81 feet

DRAFT
21 feet

PASSENGERS
490

OFFICERS
Italian

CREW
European / International

PASSENGER DECKS
8

SHIPYARD
T. Mariotti Genoa

GROSS TONNAGE
30,000

CRUISING SPEED
19.5 knots

SHIP'S REGISTRY
Bahamas

SUITE CATEGORIES:

- CATEGORY **MS**
- CATEGORY **GS**
- CATEGORY **NS**
- CATEGORY **A**
- CATEGORY **B**
- CATEGORY **C**
- CATEGORY **D**
- CATEGORY **E**
- CATEGORY **F**
- CATEGORY **G**
- CATEGORY **H**

━━━ *Adjoining Suites*

♿ *Suites 832,833,928,929
Wheelchair accessible*

● *Three passenger
capacity suites.*

DECK TWELVE

DECK ELEVEN

DECK TEN

DECK NINE

DECK EIGHT

DECK SEVEN

DECK SIX

DECK FIVE

Life on board

The Compass Rose Restaurant

Deck 5

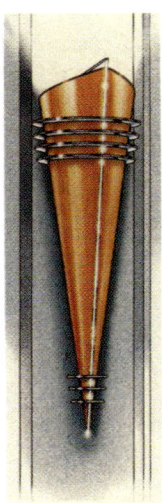

Creating a great dining establishment is no simple task. First it takes the imagination and creativity of an inspired chef. Add to this a serene setting elegantly designed to welcome diners with an ambience of taste and comfort. And finally, it requires the perseverance, knowledge and tender love of a maitre d' and staff who are totally committed to offering only the best to their appreciative clientele.

The elegant restaurant is illuminated by conical sconces springing from the walls, while a stylised compass embedded in the ceiling points the way to the tables.

Silken draperies and brocades are in soft pastels of apricot, peach, terra cotta, moss and mist, accented by alabaster and burled briar.

Thickly napped carpet and glossy marble pattern the floors.

Tables are prepared with the finest linen, crystal and silver and all the passengers benefit from the open single seating that allows them the freedom of choosing their own tablemates.

Italian and International cuisine prepared by experienced chefs offers unique and appealing menus every day.

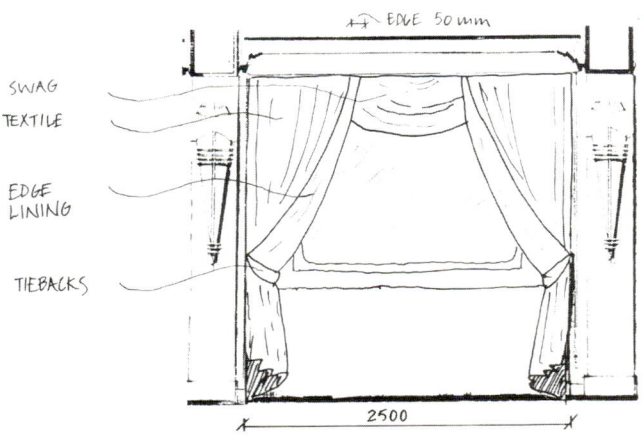

SWAG
TEXTILE
EDGE LINING
TIEBACKS
EDGE 50 mm
2500

The Casino

Deck 7

The ship's Casino offers blackjack, roulette, Caribbean stud poker and slot machines.
It is divided into two distinct but adjoining sections.
One contains the table, the other an array of slot machines.
Both sections are furnished in rich woods and damasks.

The Lido Area
Deck 10

The *Seven Seas Navigator*, with her huge and uncrowded open decks and her splendid swimming pool, provides her passengers with every opportunity to enjoy the sun or, for the more energetic, to exercise on the jogging track.

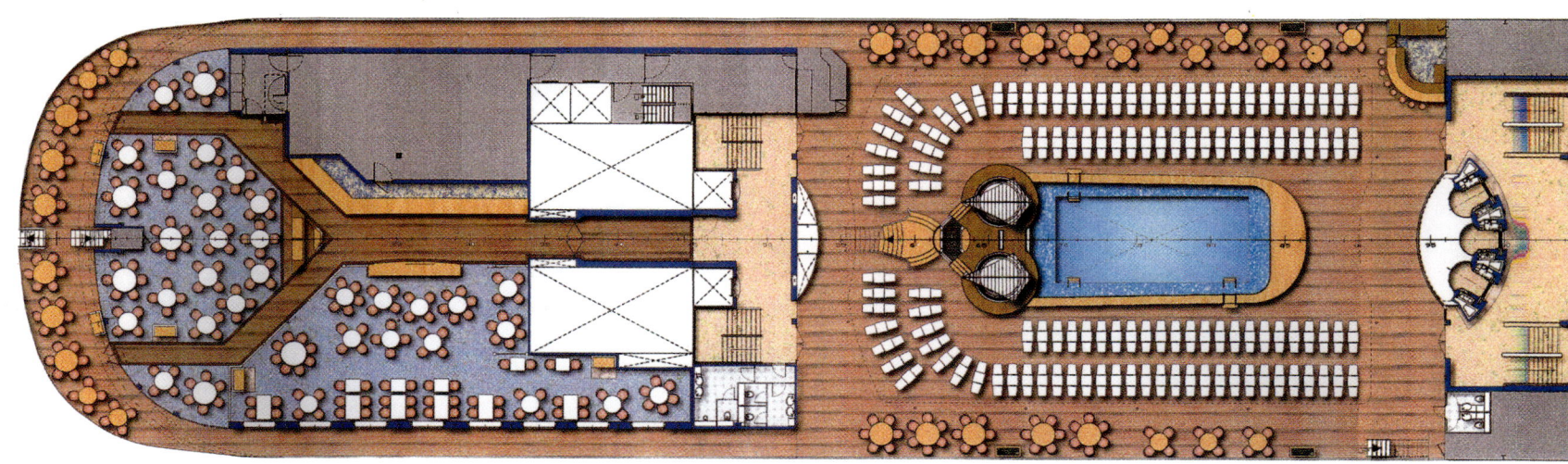

Jacuzzis, live music, a pool bar and, at night, subtle lighting add to the delights of the lido.

An evening buffet party around the
ship's swimming pool.
During special nights at sea, the lido
becomes the perfect setting for
enjoying the sea breezes,
while eating delicious
delicatessen, accompanied by soft
music provided by the ship's band;
meanwhile the twinkling stars,
reflected in the swimming pool, create
a romantic atmosphere.

The galleys of the *Seven Seas Navigator* are of the highest standard of hygiene and functionality.
Once a week red carpets are unrolled along the main galley's alleyways, tables are adorned with sumptuous buffets and
passengers are invited to admire the finest Continental fare
normally served in the Compass Rose Restaurant
and in the Portofino Grill.

Galileo's and the Vista Lounge
Decks 11 and 12

Splendid views at opposite ends of the ship. Galileo's, a comfortable bar facing over the stern, is encircled by a teak-clad balcony from which passengers may watch the ship's wake while enjoying their drinks.

The Vista Lounge, on the other hand, faces forward; during the day it is a quiet and intimate place, perfect for an early coffee or for relaxing after time spent in the adjacent Spa.

A popular feature is a screen enabling passengers to share with the officers on the bridge immediately below some of the meteorological and navigational information related to the ship's course.

During the evening, the Vista Lounge is available for private cocktail parties.

The Portofino Grill

Deck 10

For a casual breakfast or lunch, the Portofino Grill offers "al fresco" dining to the passengers as an informal alternative to the Compass Rose Restaurant. During the evening the bright room, with deck to deck glass-walls overlooking the sea, is transformed into an elegant "Trattoria", serving authentic Italian fare.

The Central Atrium

Decks 4 to 12

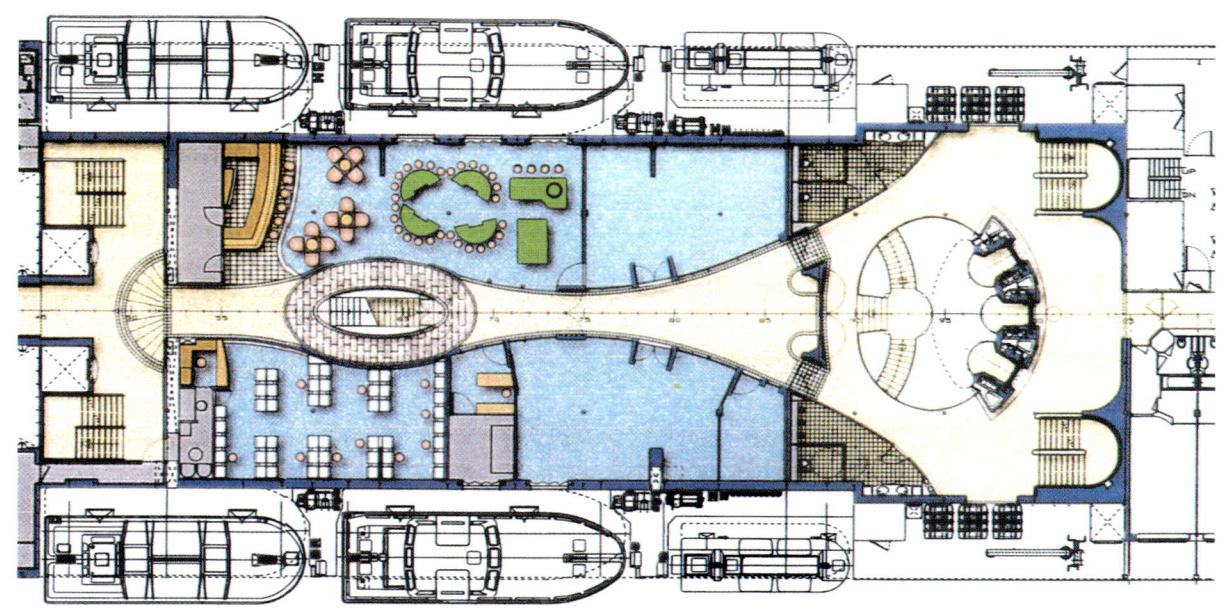

Decks 6 and 7: **the public areas**

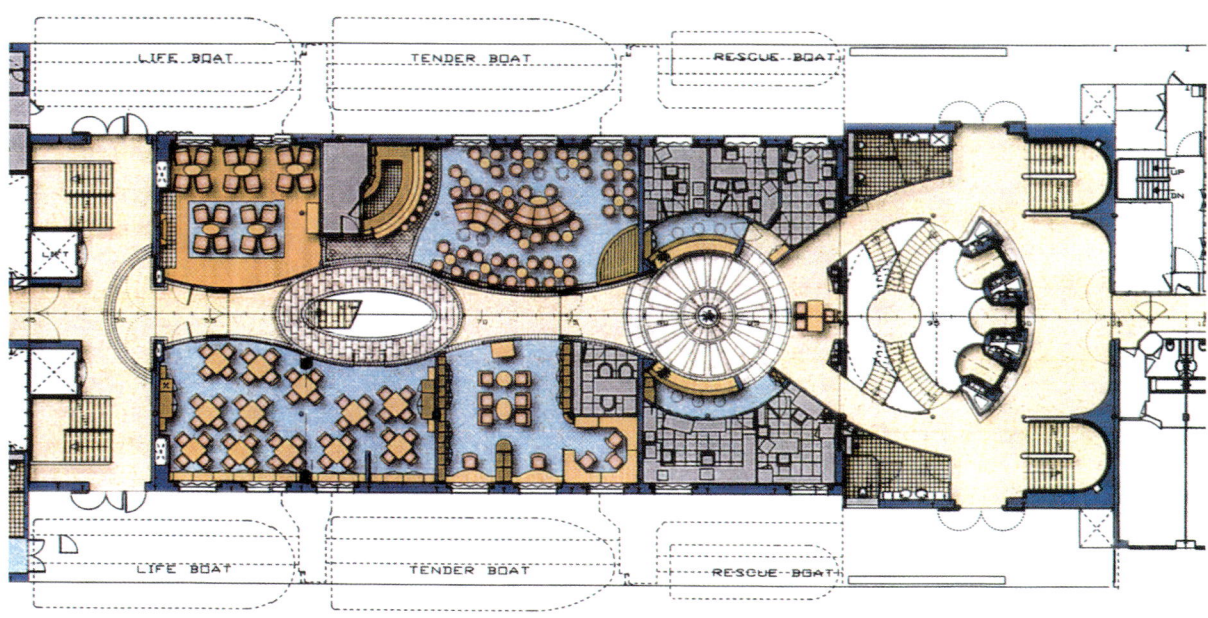

The towering Atrium is an exciting area
of vertical space at the very heart of
the ship;
it is formed by great walls
of glass and contains tall stairways
and glass-walled elevators which give
panoramic views and rise to the
uppermost decks.
Leading off it at various
levels are the decks containing
the public rooms and the
passenger accommodation.
On deck 7, *below*, is located the
Reception Desk.

83

One of the most intimate bars and rest spaces on board the vessel: the Navigator Lounge.
A quiet place, during the days at sea, where you may enjoy a drink or read a book selected from the adjacent library, accompanied by quiet piped-in music.

The Navigator Lounge
Deck 6

The arcades linking the public rooms on decks 6 and 7.
Many rich materials were used to furnish the passenger spaces of the *Seven Seas Navigator*. These include Alabaster, red Travertino and Alicante stone, Juparana marble, veneer of American cherry, solid teak and best Axminster carpet specially designed for the ship.

On deck 7, the on-board boutique offers souvenirs and a vast selection of items to make the stay on the *Seven Seas Navigator* more pleasant.

The spectacular central staircase which connects the public rooms of decks 6 and 7.

Among the other facilities offered by
the *Seven Seas Navigator* are
a well-stocked library and the Connoisseur
Club. In this
traditionally-styled room,
with its parquet floor, fireplace
and comfortable leather chairs,
guests may relax and enjoy
a fine cigar.

The Library and the Connoisseur Club

Deck 6

Dedicated enthusiasts for bridge and other games will gravitate towards the ship's CardRoom.

The Card Room

Deck 6

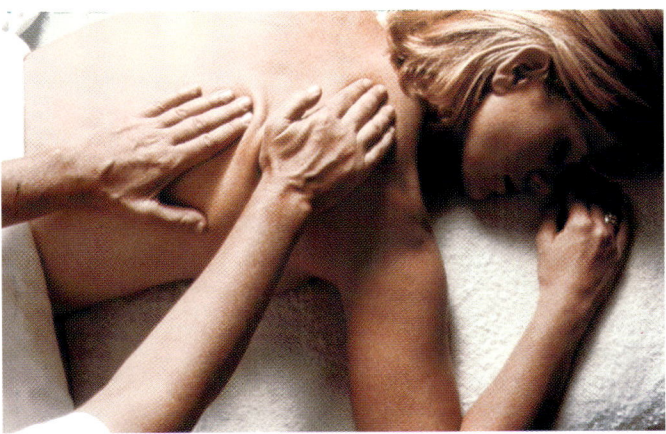

The gym, facing the sea, is fitted with the most modern and effective equipment.
After exercising, passengers can have a massage in the large and modern Spa and later relax and enjoy the seascape in the Vista Lounge.

A whole deck on *Seven Seas Navigator* is devoted to the health and well-being of the passengers.
In addition to the sauna, Turkish bath and massage rooms, guests can enjoy such specialised treatments as aromatherapy, essential oils and reflexology.

The Gymnasium and Sea Spa
Deck 12

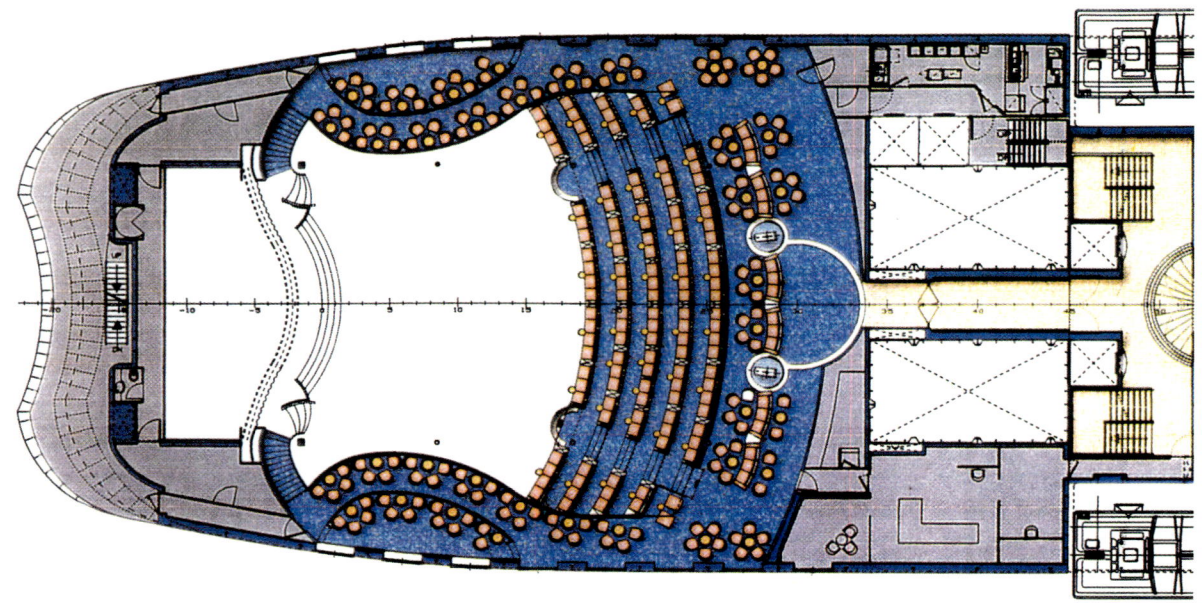

The Seven Seas Show Lounge

Decks 6 and 7

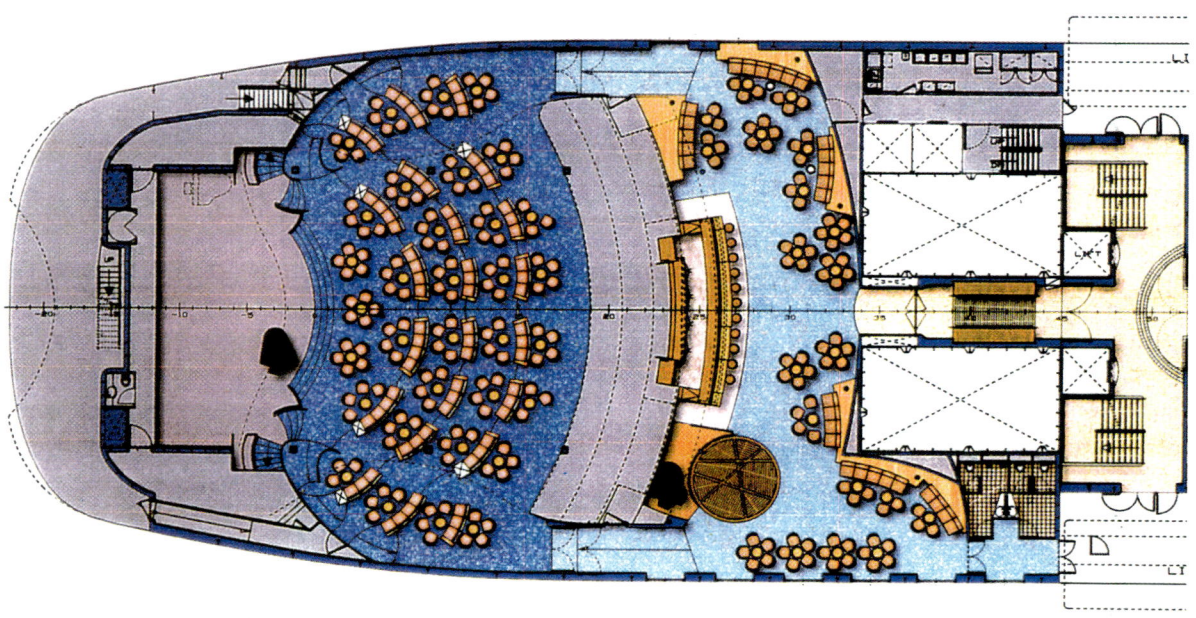

The Stars Lounge

Deck 6

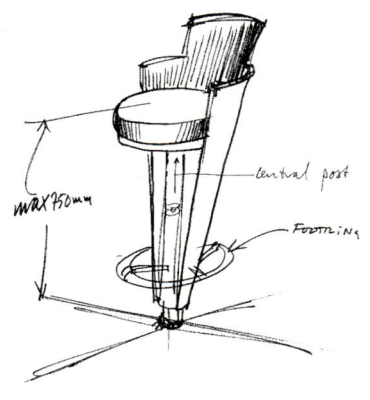

Access to the Seven Seas Lounge is through the Stars Lounge where cocktails and aperitifs are served before dinner.

Entrance to the Stars Lounge, the theatre bar, is through a corridor reminiscent of a bridge and flanked by glass and mirrors.

The two-level show lounge, known as the Seven Seas Lounge, is the venue for most of the ship's night-time entertainment. With its excellent sight-lines and well-equipped stage this large lounge is the ideal setting to enjoy the high-spirited spectacles offered by the ship's entertainers.

There are no cabins for the passengers on board the *Seven Seas Navigator*, only space-generous suites. The smallest one is more than 300 square feet, while the largest measures an enormous 1,173 sq ft, including a large balcony, clad with traditional teak wood. Damasks and silks in the shades of sand, terra-cotta and taupe surround the guest with eye-pleasing colours and body-easing comfort.

The soft fabrics are set off by warmly finished woods and floors of thick and soft carpet. Each suite boasts a European king-size bed or twin beds, separate living-room area, mini-bar stocked with select beverages, walk-in closet, TV/VCR and marble bathroom with full tub and separate shower.

All suites are outside, with sweeping views enabling guests to enjoy the seascape or to view the ports where the ship calls; 90% have private balconies. Ten suites are also interconnecting, each offering a maximum combined square footage of 1,530 ft, including the veranda. The private accommodation is typical of the expansive ambience of the entire vessel.

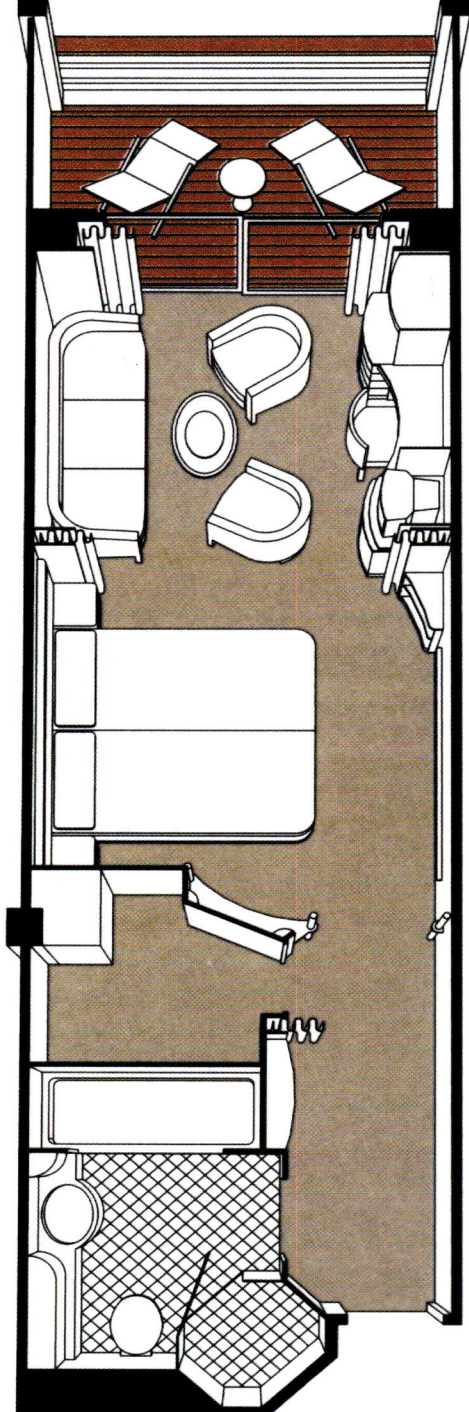

On deck 5, where the Compass Rose Restaurant is also located, there are 22 suites of the standard size, 301 square feet each. They have all the amenities of the larger ones,
including a marble-clad bathroom with separate tub and shower.

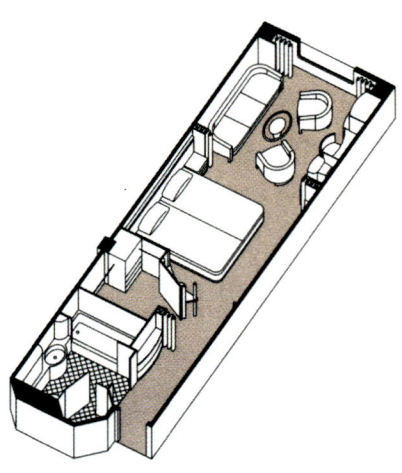

The few suites without a balcony have large windows looking out to sea. There are no internal cabins on this ship.

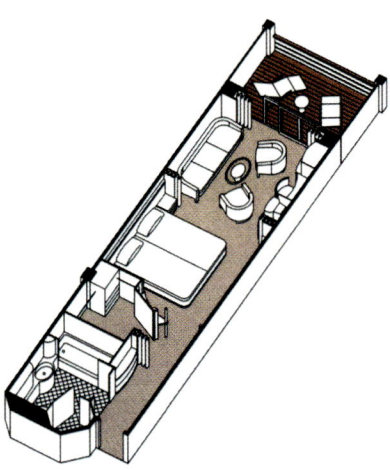

Equal in lay-out to the suites without balcony, the standard suites offer every comfort to their guests and a spacious living area where it is even possible to have meals without leaving the stateroom.

A basket of fresh fruit and a bottle of
champagne, accompanied by a fine selection
of beverages and snacks from the private
mini-bar, welcome the guests in each suite.
Private TV and VCR offer
a large selection of movies from the ship's
library, constantly updated with the latest
titles.

The Standard Suites

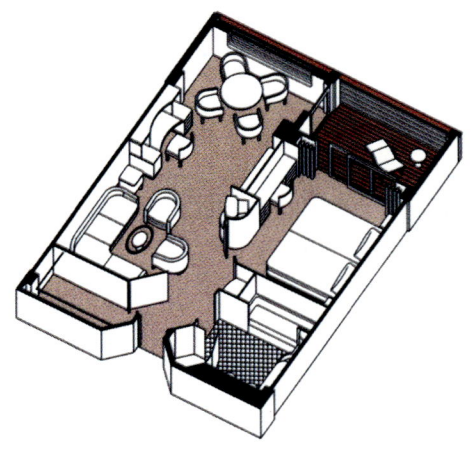

The ten Navigator suites are interconnecting and each of them has an ample surface of 448 sq ft plus 47 sq ft of veranda. The bedroom is fully independent and there is also a large walk-in closet. The full-size table permits passengers to enjoy their meals in comfort in their stateroom, using the 24-hour cabin service of the *Seven Seas Navigator*. These suites are located in the upper part of the vessel, on deck 9.

The Navigator Suites

Deck 9

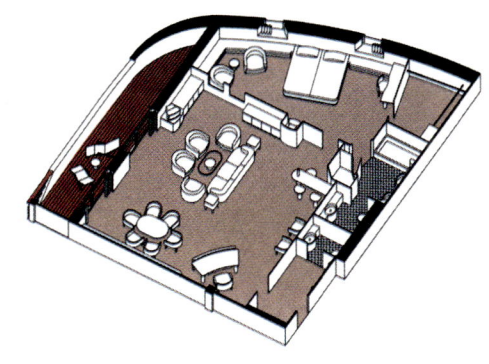

As the name itself implies, these suites, located on decks 9 and 10, are the most generous in space to be found on board, with their 1,067 sq ft of internal surface plus a huge veranda of 106 sq ft.
Two of them have side balconies while on deck 10 the veranda wraps around the whole room, offering
a privileged forward view of the sea while the ship is in motion.

The Master Suites
Deck 9 and 10

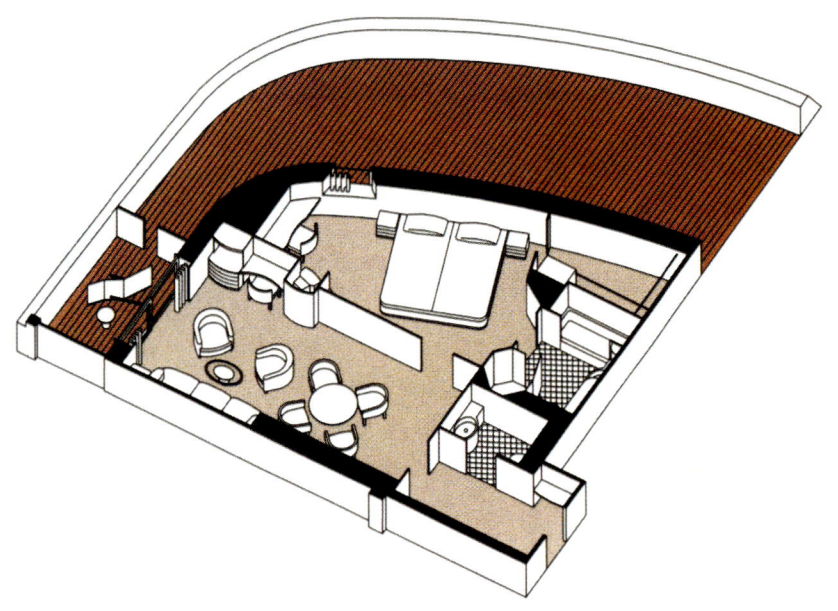

A little smaller than the Master Suites, but equally comfortable, are the Grand Suites on decks 7 and 8; They
measure 539 sq ft and furthermore have a large veranda of 200 sq ft.
Suites 800 and 801, on deck 8, have full wrap-around balconies with a
forward-facing view of the sea.

The Grand Suites
Deck 7 and 8

As can be clearly seen from this aerial photograph, tables and easy-chairs are part of the standard furnishing of each balcony; it is thus possible for those guests who prefer the intimacy of their suite to enjoy breakfast in private.

M/V Seven Seas Navigator

Length o. a.:	170.6 m (560 ft)
Length b.p.:	150.0 m (492 ft)
Breadth m.:	24.8 m (81.4 ft)
Draft:	6.9 m (23 ft)
Gross tonnage:	30,000
Net tonnage:	9,700
Displacement:	17,338 t
Deadweight:	2,581 t

International call sign: C6QS8

Passengers:	490
Crew:	400
Suites:	251
Wheelchair acc.:	4
Public lounges:	13
Restaurants:	2
Bars:	5
1 Swimming pool - 2 Jacuzzies	

Engines:

4 Diesels x 5280 kW each	
Service speed:	19.5 kn
Max speed:	21 kn
Generators:	3 x 2,120 kW
Shaft altern.:	2 x 2,500 kW
Propellers:	2 C.P.
Bow Thruster:	2 x 500kW
Stabilisers:	2 retractable fins

Acknowledgements

The author wishes to express a word of sincere gratitude to the individuals and organisations who supported and permitted the realisation of this book.

In alphabetical order they are: Ms Brina Anelli (RSSC Marketing Co-ordinator), Mr Giovanni Biasutti (First Officer), Mr Per Bjorsen (V.Ships Leisure), Mr Nello Brancaccio (photographer), Mr Arnold Brereton (V.Ships Newbuilding Department), Mr Alessandro Cane (photographer), Mr Mark Conroy (RSSC President), Mr Anthony Cooke (maritime historian and publisher), Mr Francesco Dell'Olio Lespine (graphic designer), Mr Roberto Fazi (V.Ships Newbuilding Department), Mr Vittorio Facco (V.Ships Newbuilding Department), Lord Greenway (maritime historian and photographer), Mr Hannes Lindthaller, Mr Kristen Lewis (RSSC), Mr Fausto Mazza (Staff Captain), Mr Ken Norman (V.Ships Newbuilding Department), Mr Giuseppe Repetto (photographer), Mr Enrico Repetto (maritime historian), Mr Alfredo Romeo (Master), Mr Christian Sauleau (RSSC vice-President).

Photographic credits

Giovanni Biasutti: 48, 49.

Nello Brancaccio: dustjacket (front), 21 (right), 26, 27, 28 (bottom), 34, 36, 40, 58, 63 (left), 68 (bottom), 70 (bottom), 77 (top), 78, 85 (left), 93 (top right), 94 (top), 95 (top left and bottom), 98 (bottom), 99, 102, 104, 105.

Maurizio Eliseo: 2, 6, 8,9, 10 (bottom left), 11, 12, 28 (top), 29 (centre and top), 32, 33, 44, 45, 47, 50, 53, 55, 56 (right), 59, 60, 61, 62, 63 (right), 65, 66 (top right and bottom), 67 (bottom right), 68 (top), 69, 70 (top), 71 (top right and centre right), 72, 73, 74, 75, 76, 77 (bottom), 83 (top left, top right and bottom left), 84, 85 (right), 86, 87, 88, 89 (top), 90, 93 (bottom), 94 (bottom), 97, 98 (top), 100, 101, 103.

Roberto Fazi: 15,16, 21 (top left), 30 (top).

T. Mariotti: 10 (top), 10 (centre), 18, 30 (bottom), 31 (top).

RSSC: dustjacket (back), 2 & 3, 14, 17, 64, 71 (top left), 82 (right), 89 (bottom), 91, 96.

Enrico Repetto: 31 (bottom).

Giuseppe Repetto: 24, 29 (bottom), 35, 37, 38, 39, 41, 42, 43, 46, 51, 52, 54, 56 (left), 57, 79.

Yran & Storbraaten: 19, 66 (top left), 67 (top and bottom left), 71 (bottom), 81, 82 (left), 83 (bottom right), 92, 93 (centre).

V.Ships Monaco: 21 (bottom left), 22, 23, 30.

ISBN 0 953 4291 6 4

Published January 2001

by

Carmania Press
Unit 212
Station House
49, Greenwich High Road
London SE10 8JL

PRINTED IN ITALY - LANG SRL GENOVA